Zigzag Hat,
page 21

Diagonal Stairsteps
Hat, *page 11*

Learn to Crochet
Mosaic Hats™

Have you always wanted to create beautiful crocheted colorwork but been afraid of working with more than one yarn at a time? If so, mosaic colorwork is the technique for you!

These complicated-looking patterns are created by working simple two-row stripes. On successive rows, stitches are worked into the rows below to create the intricate patterns. It's as easy as that!

With concise instructions and photos, this book will take you step by step through the creation of basic mosaic fabric. There are useful patterns for seven hats in teens', women's and men's sizes so you can showcase your new skills. No one needs to know how easy—and fun—these gorgeous hats are to make. It'll be our special secret!

Let's get started!

Table of Contents

Confetti Stripes Hat,
page 7

Byzantine Hat,
page 16

Mosaic Basics

This fascinating colorwork technique requires just one color per row and is created using simple crochet stitches. Chain-2 spaces are used as placeholders where stitches of the other color will be worked. In subsequent rows, double crochet stitches are used to cover those chain-2 spaces and add the appropriate color in the desired spot in the pattern.

Let's learn how to do mosaic colorwork while stitching the 3-in-1 mosaic pattern stitch used in the 3-in-1 Hat on page 4.

Begin with the foundation rows. They're worked once at the beginning of a project and are not repeated. The rows will each be the height of a single crochet stitch, so each one will have one chain at the beginning of the subsequent row to bring the yarn and hook up to the height required to work that row.

With gray, chain a multiple of 4.

Foundation row 1 (RS): Sc in 2nd ch from hook *(see Photo 1)* and in each ch across, turn.

Foundation row 2 is a wrong-side row.

Foundation row 2 (WS): Ch 1, sc in first sc *(see Photo 2)* and in each sc across *(see Photo 3)*, change color to magenta in last st, turn.

Photo 1

Photo 2

Photo 3

To change color at the end of the row, work the last stitch to the last yarn over *(2 loops on the hook)*, drop gray, leaving a 6-inch tail, draw magenta through the 2 loops *(see Photo 4)*. One loop of magenta is on the hook and now you're ready to begin the next row.

Photo 4

Foundation row 3 (RS): Ch 1, sc in each of first 3 sc *(see Photo 5)*, *ch 2, sk next sc, sc in each of next 3 sc *(see Photo 6)*, rep from * across, turn.

Photo 5

Photo 6

Foundation row 4 (WS): Ch 1, sc in each of first 3 sc *(see Photo 7)*, *ch 2, sk next ch-2 sp, sc in each of next 3 sc, rep from * across, change color to gray, turn.

To minimize the number of yarn tails that will need to be woven in at the end of a mosaic project, there's no need to cut the yarn at the end of each two-row stripe. Instead, carry the yarn loosely up the wrong

Photo 7

side of the fabric until it is used again *(see Photo 8)*.
Hint: *If you twist the yarns in opposite directions each time you change color (grabbing the new yarn from above this time and from below the next time), you'll avoid tangling the yarns as you go!*

Photo 8

Now begin the main pattern with row 1 and gray:

Row 1 (RS): Ch 1, sc in first sc, *ch 2, sk next sc, sc in next sc**, working in front of ch-2 sps of previous 2 rows, dc in next sk st 3 rows below *(see Photo 9)*, sc in next sc *(see Photo 10)*, rep from * across, ending last rep at **, turn.

Photo 9

Photo 10

As you continue with the pattern, working rows 2–4, be sure to skip the next stitch or chain space for each chain-2 made and always work your double crochet stitches in front of the chain-2 spaces of the previous two rows.

Row 2: Ch 1, sc in first sc, *ch 2, sk next ch-2 sp**, sc in each of next 3 sts, rep from * across, ending last rep at **, sc in last sc, change color to magenta, turn.

Row 3: Ch 1, sc in first sc, *dc in next sk st 3 rows below, sc in next sc**, ch 2, sk next sc, sc in next sc, rep from * across, ending last rep at **, turn.

Row 4: Ch 1, sc in each of first 3 sc, *ch 2, sk next ch-2 sp, sc in each of next 3 sc, rep from * across, change color to gray, turn.

At the end of row 4, begin again with row 1—not with the foundation rows *(see Photo 11)*.

Repeat rows 1–4 for pattern.

Photo 11

After you've completed all repeats of rows 1–4, you'll need to work 2 last rows that omit the chain-2 spaces to avoid having holes in the fabric. With gray on your hook, continue as follows:

Next row (RS): Ch 1, sc in each of first 3 sc, *dc into the next sk st 3 rows below, sc in each of next 3 sc *(see Photo 12)*, rep from * across, turn.

Last row: Ch 1, sc in each st across *(see Photo 13)*. Fasten off. ●

Photo 12

Photo 13

3-in-1 Hat

Skill Level

 EASY

Finished Sizes

Instructions given fit teen; changes for woman and man are in [ ].

Finished Measurements

Circumference: 18 [20½, 23] inches

Length: 10 [11, 11½] inches tall

Materials

- Premier Yarns Deborah Norville Everyday Soft Worsted medium (worsted) weight acrylic yarn (4 oz/203 yds/113g per ball):
  1 [1, 2] ball(s) #1023 mist
  1 ball #1021 magenta
- Size H/8/5mm crochet hook or size needed to obtain gauge
- Tapestry needle

Gauge

Ribbing: 4 sc = 1 inch; 13 rows = 4 inches

Body: 13 sts = 4 inches; 18 rows = 4 inches

Pattern Notes

Weave in ends as work progresses.

Work all double crochet stitches in front of chain-2 spaces of previous 2 rows throughout.

Pattern Stitch

3-in-1 Pattern

Row 1 (RS): Ch 1, sc in first sc, *ch 2, sk next sc, sc in next sc**, **working in front of ch-2 sps of previous 2 rows** *(see Pattern Notes)*, dc in next sk sc 3 rows below, sc in next sc, rep from * across, ending last

rep at **, turn. *(30 [34, 38] sc, 14 [16, 18] dc, 15 [17, 19] ch-2 sps)*

Row 2: Ch 1, sc in first sc, *ch 2, sk next ch-2 sp**, sc in each of next 3 sts, rep from * across, ending last rep at **, sc in last sc, change color to magenta, turn. *(44 [54, 64] sc, 15 [17, 19] ch-2 sps)*

Row 3: Ch 1, sc in first sc, *dc in next sk sc 3 rows below, sc in next sc**, ch 2, sk next sc, sc in next sc, rep from * across, ending last rep at **, turn. *(30 [34, 38] sc, 14 [16, 18] dc, 15 [17, 19] ch-2 sps)*

Row 4: Ch 1, sc in each of first 3 sc, *ch 2, sk next ch-2 sp, sc in each of next 3 sc, rep from * across, change color to mist, turn. *(44 [54, 64] sc, 15 [17, 19] ch-2 sps)*

Rep rows 1–4 for pattern.

Hat

Ribbing

Row 1 (RS): With mist, ch 8 [9, 9], sc in 2nd ch from hook and in each ch across, turn. *(7 [8, 8] sc)*

Row 2: Ch 1, sc in **back lp** *(see Stitch Guide)* of each sc across, turn.

Rep row 2 until Ribbing measures 17 [19½, 22] inches, slightly stretched. Do not fasten off.

Body

Foundation row 1 (RS): With RS facing and working in ends of rows, ch 1, work 59 [67, 75] sc evenly sp across, turn. *(59 [67, 75] sc)*

Foundation row 2: Ch 1, sc in each sc across, **change color** *(see Stitch Guide)* in last sc to magenta, turn.

Foundation row 3: Ch 1, sc in each of first 3 sc, *ch 2, sk next sc, sc in each of next 3 sc, rep from * across, turn. *(44 [54, 64] sc, 15 [17, 19] ch-2 sps)*

Foundation row 4: Ch 1, sc in each of first 3 sc, *ch 2, sk next ch-2 sp, sc in each of next 3 sc, rep from * across, change color to mist, turn.

Next rows: Work in **3-in-1 Pattern** *(see Pattern Stitch)* until piece measures approximately 7 [8, 8] inches from bottom edge of Ribbing, ending at row 4.

Next row (RS): Ch 1, sc in each of first 3 sc, *dc in next sk sc 3 rows below, sc in each of next 3 sc, rep from * across, turn.

Crown

Next row: Ch 1, **sc dec** *(see Stitch Guide)* in first 2 sc, *sc in each of next 18 [15, 13] sts, sc dec in next 2 sts, rep from * 1 [2, 3] time(s), sc in each rem st, turn. *(56 [63, 70] sc)*

Next row: Ch 1, sc in each sc across, turn.

Rep last row until piece measures approximately 8 [9, 9½] inches from bottom edge of Ribbing or 2 inches less than desired height.

Next row (dec): Ch 1, sc dec in first 2 sc, sc in each of next 5 sc, *sc dec in next 2 sc, sc in each of next 5 sc, rep from * across, turn. *(48 [54, 60] sc)*

Next row (dec): Ch 1, sc dec in first 2 sc, sc in each of next 4 sc, *sc dec in next 2 sc, sc in each of next 4 sc, rep from * across, turn. *(40 [45, 50] sc)*

Next row (dec): Ch 1, sc dec in first 2 sc, sc in each of next 3 sc, *sc dec in next 2 sc, sc in each of next 3 sc, rep from * across, turn. *(32 [36, 40] sc)*

Next row (dec): Ch 1, sc dec in first 2 sc, sc in each of next 2 sc, *sc dec in next 2 sc, sc in each of next 2 sc, rep from * across, turn. *(24 [27, 30] sc)*

Next row (dec): Ch 1, sc dec in first 2 sc, sc in next sc, *sc dec in next 2 sc, sc in next sc, rep from * across, turn. *(16 [18, 20] sc)*

Last row (dec): Ch 1, sc dec in first 2 sc, sc in next sc, *sc dec in next 2 sc, sc in next sc, rep from * across, turn. Leaving an 8-inch tail, fasten off. *(8 [9, 10] sc)*

Finishing

Weave tail through last row and pull tightly to secure. Sew back seam. ●

Designer's Tip

It's easy to customize these hats for a trendy slouchy look. Just work more rows of single crochet before starting the crown decreases!

Confetti Stripes Hat

Skill Level

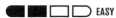 EASY

Finished Sizes

Instructions given fit teen; changes for woman and man are in [ ].

Finished Measurements

Circumference: 18 [20½, 23] inches

Length: 10 [11, 11½] inches tall

Materials

- Premier Yarns Deborah Norville Everyday Soft Worsted medium (worsted) weight acrylic yarn (4 oz/203 yds/113g per ball):
  1 [1, 2] ball(s) #1030 glass
  1 ball #1017 azure
- Size H/8/5mm crochet hook or size needed to obtain gauge
- Tapestry needle

Gauge

Ribbing: 4 sc = 1 inch; 13 rows = 4 inches

Body: 13 sts = 4 inches; 18 rows = 4 inches

Pattern Notes

Weave in ends as work progresses.

Work all double crochet stitches in front of chain-2 spaces of previous 2 rows throughout.

Pattern Stitch

Confetti Stripes Pattern

Row 1 (RS): Ch 1, sc in first sc, ***working in front of ch-2 sps of previous 2 rows** (see Pattern Notes), dc in next sk sc 3 rows below**, ch 2, sk next sc, sc in each of next 2 sc, rep from * across, ending last rep at **, sc in last sc, turn. (30 [34, 38] sc, 15 [17, 19] dc, 14 [16, 18] ch-2 sps)

Row 2: Ch 1, sc in each of first 3 sts, *sc in next sc, ch 2, sk next ch-2 sp, sc in each of next 2 sts, rep from * across, change color to azure, turn. (45 [51, 57] sc, 14 [16, 18] ch-2 sps)

Row 3: Ch 1, sc in first sc, *ch 2, sk next sc, dc in next sk sc 3 rows below, sc in each of next 2 sc, rep from * across to last 2 sc, ch 2, sk next sc, sc in last sc, turn. (30 [34, 38] sc, 14 [16, 18] dc, 15 [17, 19] ch-2 sps)

Row 4: Ch 1, sc in first sc, *ch 2, sk next ch-2 sp, sc in each of next 3 sts, rep from * across to last ch-2 sp, ch 2, sk last ch-2 sp, sc in last sc, change color to glass, turn. (44 [50, 56] sc, 15 [17, 19] ch-2 sps)

Row 5: Ch 1, sc in first sc, dc in next sk sc 3 rows below, *sc in each of next 2 sc, ch 2, sk next sc, dc in next sk sc 3 rows below, rep from * across to last sc, sc in last sc, turn. (30 [34, 38] sc, 15 [17, 19] dc, 14 [16, 18] ch-2 sps)

Row 6: Ch 1, sc in each of first 2 sts, *ch 2, sk next ch-2 sp, sc in each of next 3 sts, rep from * across to last sc, sc in last sc, change color to azure, turn. (45 [51, 57] sc, 14 [16, 18] ch-2 sps)

Row 7: Ch 1, sc in first sc, *ch 2, sk next sc, sc in each of next 2 sc, dc in next sk sc 3 rows below, rep from * across to last 2 sc, ch 2, sk next sc, sc in last sc, turn. (30 [34, 38] sc, 14 [16, 18] dc, 15 [17, 19] ch-2 sps)

Row 8: Rep row 4.

Rep rows 1–8 for pattern.

Hat

Ribbing

Row 1 (RS): With glass, ch 8 [9, 9], sc in 2nd ch from hook and in each ch across, turn. (7 [8, 8] sc)

Row 2: Ch 1, sc in **back lp** (see Stitch Guide) of each sc across, turn.

Rep row 2 until Ribbing measures 17 [19½, 22] inches, slightly stretched. Do not fasten off.

Body

Foundation row 1 (RS): With RS facing and working in ends of rows, ch 1, work 59 [67, 75] sc evenly sp across, turn. *(59 [67, 75] sc)*

Foundation row 2: Ch 1, sc in each sc across, turn, **change color** *(see Stitch Guide)* in last sc to azure. *(44 [54, 64] sc, 15 [17, 19] ch-2 sps)*

Foundation row 3: Ch 1, sc in first sc, *ch 2, sk next sc**, sc in each of next 3 sc, rep from * across, ending last rep at **, sc in last sc, turn. *(44 [54, 64] sc, 15 [17, 19] ch-2 sps)*

Foundation row 4: Ch 1, sc in first sc, *ch 2, sk next ch-2 sp**, sc in each of next 3 sc, rep from * across, ending last rep at **, sc in last sc, change color to glass, turn.

Next rows: Work in **Confetti Stripes Pattern** *(see Pattern Stitch)* until piece measures approximately 7 [8, 8] inches from bottom edge of Ribbing, ending at row 4.

Next row (RS): Ch 1, sc in first sc, dc in next sk sc 3 rows below, *sc in each of next 3 sc, dc in next sk sc 3 rows below, rep from * across to last sc, sc in last sc, turn.

Crown

Size Teen Only

Next row: Ch 1, **sc dec** *(see Stitch Guide)* in first 2 sts, *sc in each of next 18 sts, sc dec in next 2 sts, rep from * once, sc in each rem st, turn. *(56 sc)*

Next row: Ch 1, sc in each sc across, turn.

Rep last row until piece measures approximately 8 inches from bottom edge of Ribbing or 2 inches less than desired height.

Sizes Woman & Man Only

Next row: Ch 1, sc in each sc across, turn. *([67, 75] sc)*

Rep last row until piece measures approximately [9, 9½] inches from bottom edge of Ribbing or 2 inches less than desired height.

Next row: Ch 1, **sc dec** *(see Stitch Guide)* in first 2 sc, *sc in each of next [15, 13] sts, sc dec in next 2 sc, rep from * [2, 3] times, sc in each rem st, turn. *([63, 70] sc)*

All Sizes

Next row (dec): Ch 1, sc dec in first 2 sc, sc in each of next 5 sc, *sc dec in next 2 sc, sc in each of next 5 sc, rep from * across, turn. *(48 [54, 60] sc)*

Next row (dec): Ch 1, sc dec in first 2 sc, sc in each of next 4 sc, *sc dec in next 2 sc, sc in each of next 4 sc, rep from * across, turn. *(40 [45, 50] sc)*

Next row (dec): Ch 1, sc dec in first 2 sc, sc in each of next 3 sc, *sc dec in next 2 sc, sc in each of next 3 sc, rep from * across, turn. *(32 [36, 40] sc)*

Next row (dec): Ch 1, sc dec in first 2 sc, sc in each of next 2 sc, *sc dec in next 2 sc, sc in each of next 2 sc, rep from * across, turn. *(24 [27, 30] sc)*

Next row (dec): Ch 1, sc dec in first 2 sc, sc in next sc, *sc dec in next 2 sc, sc in next sc, rep from * across, turn. *(16 [18, 20] sc)*

Last row (dec): Ch 1, sc dec in first 2 sc, sc in next sc, *sc dec in next 2 sc, sc in next sc, rep from * across, turn. Leaving an 8-inch tail, fasten off. *(8 [9, 10] sc)*

Finishing

Weave tail through last row and pull tightly to secure. Sew back seam. ●

Diagonal Stairsteps Hat

Skill Level
 EASY

Finished Sizes
Instructions given fit teen; changes for woman and man are in [ ].

Finished Measurements
Circumference: 18 [20½, 23] inches

Length: 10 [11, 11½] inches tall

Materials
- Premier Yarns Deborah Norville Everyday Heathers medium (worsted) weight acrylic yarn (3½ oz/180 yds/100g per ball):
    1 [1, 2] ball(s) #0009 charcoal heather
    1 ball #0008 grey heather
- Size H/8/5mm crochet hook or size needed to obtain gauge
- Tapestry needle

4 MEDIUM

Gauge
Ribbing: 4 sc = 1 inch; 13 rows = 4 inches

Body: 13 sts = 4 inches, 18 rows = 4 inches

Pattern Notes
Weave in ends as work progresses.

Work all double crochet stitches in front of chain-2 spaces of previous 2 rows throughout.

Pattern Stitch
Diagonal Stairsteps Pattern

Row 1 (RS): Ch 1, sc in first sc, *ch 2, sk next sc**, sc in each of next 2 sc, **working in front of ch-2 sps of previous 2 rows** (see Pattern Notes), dc in next sk sc 3 rows below, sc in next sc, rep from * across, ending last rep at **, sc in last sc, turn. (30 [34, 38] sc, 14 [16, 18] dc, 15 [17, 19] ch-2 sps)

Row 2: Ch 1, sc in first sc, *ch 2, sk next ch-2 sp**, sc in each of next 3 sts, rep from * across, ending last rep at **, sc in last sc, change color to grey, turn. (44 [54, 64] sc, 15 [17, 19] ch-2 sps)

Row 3: Ch 1, sc in first sc, *dc in next sk sc 3 rows below**, ch 2, sk next sc, sc in each of next 2 sc, rep from * across, ending last rep at **, sc in last sc, turn. (30 [34, 38] sc, 15 [17, 19] dc, 14 [16, 18] ch-2 sps)

Row 4: Ch 1, sc in each of first 4 sc, *ch 2, sk next ch-2 sp**, sc in each of next 3 sc, rep from * across, ending last rep at **, sc in each of last 2 sc, change color to charcoal, turn. (45 [51, 57] sc, 14 [16, 18] ch-2 sps)

Row 5: Ch 1, sc in each of first 2 sts, *dc in next sk sc 3 rows below, ch 2, sk next sc, sc in each of next 2 sts, rep from * across to last sc, sc in last sc, turn. (31 [35, 39] sc, 14 [16, 18] dc, 14 [16, 18] ch-2 sps)

Row 6: Ch 1, sc in each of first 3 sts, *ch 2, sk next sc, sc in each of next 3 sts, rep from * across, change color to grey, turn. (45 [51, 57] sc, 14 [16, 18] ch-2 sps)

Row 7: Ch 1, sc in each of first 3 sc, *dc in next sk sc 3 rows below, ch 2, sk next sc, sc in each of next 2 sc, rep from * across, turn. (31 [35, 39] sc, 14 [16, 18] dc, 14 [16, 18] ch-2 sps)

Row 8: Ch 1, sc in each of first 2 sc, *ch 2, sk next ch-2 sp, sc in each of next 3 sc, rep from * across to last sc, sc in last sc, change color to charcoal, turn. (45 [51, 57] sc, 14 [16, 18] ch-2 sps)

Rep rows 1–8 for pattern.

Hat

Ribbing
Row 1 (RS): With charcoal, ch 8 [9, 9], sc in 2nd ch from hook and in each ch across, turn. (7 [8, 8] sc)

Row 2: Ch 1, sc in **back lp** *(see Stitch Guide)* of each sc across, turn.

Rep row 2 until Ribbing measures 17 [19½, 22] inches, slightly stretched. Do not fasten off.

Body

Foundation row 1 (RS): With RS facing and working in ends of rows, ch 1, work 59 [67, 75] sc evenly sp across, turn. *(59 [67, 75] sc)*

Foundation row 2: Ch 1, sc in each sc across, **change color** *(see Stitch Guide)* in last sc to grey, turn.

Foundation row 3 (RS): Ch 1, sc in first sc, sc in each of next 3 sc, *ch 2, sk next sc, sc in each of next 3 sc, rep from * across to last 3 sc, ch 2, sk next sc, sc in each of last 2 sc, turn. *(45 [51, 57] sc, 14 [16, 18] ch-2 sps)*

Foundation row 4: Ch 1, sc in each of first 2 sc, *ch 2, sk next ch-2 sp, sc in each of next 3 sc, rep from * across to last sc, sc in last sc, change color to charcoal, turn.

Next rows: Work in **Diagonal Stairsteps Pattern** *(see Pattern Stitch)* until piece measures approximately 7 [8, 8] inches from bottom edge of Ribbing, ending at row 4.

Next row (RS): Ch 1, sc in each of first 2 sc, *dc in next sk sc 3 rows below, sc in each of next 3 sc, rep from * across to last sc, sc in last sc, turn. *(45 [51, 57] sc, 14 [16, 18] dc)*

Crown

Size Teen Only
Next row: Ch 1, **sc dec** *(see Stitch Guide)* in first 2 sts, *sc in each of next 18 sts, sc dec in next 2 sts, rep from * once, sc in each rem st, turn. *(56 sc)*

Next row: Ch 1, sc in each sc across, turn.

Rep last row until piece measures approximately 8 inches from bottom edge of Ribbing or 2 inches less than desired height.

Sizes Woman & Man Only
Next row: Ch 1, sc in each sc across, turn. *([67, 75] sc)*

Rep last row until piece measures approximately [9, 9½] inches from bottom edge of Ribbing or 2 inches less than desired height.

Next row: Ch 1, **sc dec** *(see Stitch Guide)* in first 2 sc, *sc in each of next [15, 13] sts, sc dec in next 2 sc, rep from * [2, 3] times, sc in each rem st, turn. *([63, 70] sc)*

All Sizes
Next row (dec): Ch 1, sc dec in first 2 sc, sc in each of next 5 sc, *sc dec in next 2 sc, sc in each of next 5 sc, rep from * across, turn. *(48 [54, 60] sc)*

Next row (dec): Ch 1, sc dec in first 2 sc, sc in each of next 4 sc, *sc dec in next 2 sc, sc in each of next 4 sc, rep from * across, turn. *(40 [45, 50] sc)*

Next row (dec): Ch 1, sc dec in first 2 sc, sc in each of next 3 sc, *sc dec in next 2 sc, sc in each of next 3 sc, rep from * across, turn. *(32 [36, 40] sc)*

Next row (dec): Ch 1, sc dec in first 2 sc, sc in each of next 2 sc, *sc dec in next 2 sc, sc in each of next 2 sc, rep from * across, turn. *(24 [27, 30] sc)*

Next row (dec): Ch 1, sc dec in first 2 sc, sc in next sc, *sc dec in next 2 sc, sc in next sc, rep from * across, turn. *(16 [18, 20] sc)*

Last row (dec): Ch 1, sc dec in first 2 sc, sc in next sc, *sc dec in next 2 sc, sc in next sc, rep from * across, turn. Leaving an 8-inch tail, fasten off. *(8 [9, 10] sc)*

Finishing
Weave tail through last row and pull tightly to secure. Sew back seam. ●

Dotted Stripes Hat

Skill Level

 **EASY**

Finished Sizes

Instructions given fit teen; changes for woman and man are in [ ].

Finished Measurements

Circumference: 18 [20½, 23] inches

Length: 10 [11, 11½] inches tall

Materials

- Premier Yarns Deborah Norville Everyday Soft Worsted medium (worsted) weight acrylic yarn (4 oz/203 yds/113g per ball):
  1 [1, 2] ball(s) #1002 cream
  1 ball #1012 black
- Size H/8/5mm crochet hook or size needed to obtain gauge
- Tapestry needle

Gauge

Ribbing: 4 sc = 1 inch, 13 rows = 4 inches

Body: 13 sts = 4 inches, 18 rows = 4 inches

Pattern Notes

Weave in ends as work progresses.

Work all double crochet stitches in front of chain-2 spaces of previous 2 rows throughout.

Pattern Stitch

Dotted Stripes Pattern

Row 1 (RS): Ch 1, sc in each sc across, turn.

Row 2: Rep row 1, change color to cream.

Row 3: Ch 1, sc in each of first 2 sc, *ch 2, sk next sc, sc in next sc, rep from * across to last sc, sc in last sc, turn. *(31 [35, 39] sc, 28 [32, 36] ch-2 sps)*

Row 4: Ch 1, sc in each of first 2 sc, *ch 2, sk next ch-2 sp, sc in next sc, rep from * across to last sc, sc in last sc, change color to black, turn.

Row 5: Ch 1, sc in each of first 2 sc, ***working in front of ch-2 sps of previous 2 rows** (see Pattern Notes), dc in next sk sc 3 rows below, sc in next sc, rep from * across to last sc, sc in last sc, turn. *(31 [35, 39] sc, 28 [32, 36] dc)*

Row 6: Rep row 2. *(59 [67, 75] sc)*

Rows 7 & 8: [Rep row 1] twice, at the end of row 8, change color to black.

Row 9: Ch 1, sc in first sc, *ch 2, sk next sc**, sc in next sc, rep from * across, ending last rep at **, sc in last sc, turn. *(30 [34, 38] sc, 29 [33, 37] ch-2 sps)*

Row 10: Ch 1, sc in first sc, *ch 2, sk next ch-2 sp, sc in next sc, rep from * across, change color to cream, turn.

Row 11: Ch 1, sc in first sc, *dc in next sk sc 3 rows below, sc in next sc, rep from * across, turn. *(30 [34, 38] sc, 29 [33, 37] dc)*

Row 12: Rep row 1, change color to black.

Rep rows 1–12 for pattern.

Hat

Ribbing
Row 1 (RS): With cream, ch 8 [9, 9], sc in 2nd ch from hook and in each ch across, turn. *(7 [8, 8] sc)*

Row 2: Ch 1, sc in **back lp** *(see Stitch Guide)* of each sc across, turn.

Rep row 2 until Ribbing measures 17 [19½, 22] inches, slightly stretched. Do not fasten off.

Body
Foundation row 1 (RS): With RS facing and working in ends of rows, ch 1, work 59 [67, 75] sc evenly sp across, turn. *(59 [67, 75] sc)*

Foundation row 2: Ch 1, sc in each sc across, **change color** *(see Stitch Guide)* in last sc to black, turn.

Next rows: Work in **Dotted Stripes Pattern** *(see Pattern Stitch)* until piece measures approximately 7½ [9, 9] inches from bottom edge of Ribbing, ending at row 8 [2, 2].

Note: *If ending at row 8, do not change color.*

Crown
Next row: Ch 1, sc in each sc across, turn. *(59 [67, 75] sc)*

Rep last row until piece measures approximately 8 [9, 9½] inches from bottom edge of Ribbing or 2 inches less than desired height.

Next row: Ch 1, **sc dec** *(see Stitch Guide)* in first 2 sc, *sc in each of next 18 [15, 13] sts, sc dec in next 2 sts, rep from * 1 [2, 3] time(s), sc in each rem st, turn. *(56 [63, 70] sc)*

Next row (dec): Ch 1, sc dec in first 2 sc, sc in each of next 5 sc, *sc dec in next 2 sc, sc in each of next 5 sc, rep from * across, turn. *(48 [54, 60] sc)*

Next row (dec): Ch 1, sc dec in first 2 sc, sc in each of next 4 sc, *sc dec in next 2 sc, sc in each of next 4 sc, rep from * across, turn. *(40 [45, 50] sc)*

Next row (dec): Ch 1, sc dec in first 2 sc, sc in each of next 3 sc, *sc dec in next 2 sc, sc in each of next 3 sc, rep from * across, turn. *(32 [36, 40] sc)*

Next row (dec): Ch 1, sc dec in first 2 sc, sc in each of next 2 sc, *sc dec in next 2 sc, sc in each of next 2 sc, rep from * across, turn. *(24 [27, 30] sc)*

Next row (dec): Ch 1, sc dec in first 2 sc, sc in next sc, *sc dec in next 2 sc, sc in next sc, rep from * across, turn. *(16 [18, 20] sc)*

Last row (dec): Ch 1, sc dec in first 2 sc, sc in next sc, *sc dec in next 2 sc, sc in next sc, rep from * across, turn. Leaving an 8-inch tail, fasten off. *(8 [9, 10] sc)*

Finishing
Weave tail through last row and pull tightly to secure. Sew back seam. ●

Byzantine Hat

Skill Level
 ■■□□ EASY

Finished Sizes
Instructions given fit teen; changes for woman and man are in [ ].

Finished Measurements
Circumference: 18 [20½, 23] inches

Length: 10 [11, 11½] inches tall

Materials

- Premier Yarns Deborah Norville Everyday Heathers medium (worsted) weight acrylic yarn (3½ oz/180 yds/100g per ball):
    1 [1, 2] ball(s) #0011 wine heather
    1 ball #0013 fog heather
- Size H/8/5mm crochet hook or size needed to obtain gauge
- Tapestry needle

Gauge
Ribbing: 4 sc = 1 inch; 13 rows = 4 inches

Body: 13 sts = 4 inches; 18 rows = 4 inches

Pattern Notes
Weave in ends as work progresses.

Work all double crochet stitches in front of chain-2 spaces of previous 2 rows throughout.

Hat

Ribbing
Row 1 (RS): With wine heather, ch 8 [9, 9], sc in 2nd ch from hook and in each ch across, turn. *(7 [8, 8] sc)*

Row 2: Ch 1, sc in **back lp** *(see Stitch Guide)* of each sc across, turn.

Rep row 2 until Ribbing measures 17 [19½, 22] inches, slightly stretched. Do not fasten off.

Body
Foundation row 1 (RS): With RS facing and working in ends of rows, ch 1, work 59 [67, 75] sc evenly sp across, turn. *(59 [67, 75] sc)*

Foundation row 2: Ch 1, sc in each sc across, **change color** *(see Stitch Guide)* in last sc to fog heather, turn.

Row 1 (RS): Ch 1, sc in each of first 3 sc, *ch 2, sk next sc, sc in each of next 3 sc, rep from * across, turn. *(45 [51, 57] sc, 14 [16, 18] ch-2 sps)*

Row 2: Ch 1, sc in each of first 3 sc, *ch 2, sk next ch-2 sp, sc in each of next 3 sc, rep from * across, change color to wine heather, turn.

Row 3: Ch 1, sc in each of first 3 sc, ***working in front of ch-2 sps of previous 2 rows** *(see Pattern Notes)*, dc in next sk sc 3 rows below, ch 2, sk next sc, sc in next sc, ch 2, sk next sc, dc in next sk sc 3 rows below, sc in each of next 3 sc, rep from * across, turn. *(31 [35, 39] sc, 14 [16, 18] dc, 14 [16, 18] ch-2 sps)*

Row 4: Ch 1, sc in first sc, *sc in each of next 3 sts, ch 2, sk next ch-2 sp, sc in next sc, ch 2, sk next ch-2 sp, sc in each of next 2 sts, rep from * across to last 2 sc, sc in each of last 2 sc, change color to fog heather, turn. *(45 [51, 57] sc, 14 [16, 18] ch-2 sps)*

Row 5: Ch 1, sc in first sc, *ch 2, sk next sc, sc in each of next 2 sc, dc in next sk sc 3 rows below, ch 2, sk next sc, dc in next sk sc 3 rows below, sc in each of next 2 sc, rep from * across to last 2 sc, ch 2, sk next sc, sc in last sc, turn. *(30 [34, 38] sc, 14 [16, 18] dc, 15 [17, 19] ch-2 sps)*

Row 6: Ch 1, sc in first sc, *ch 2, sk next ch-2 sp, sc in each of next 3 st, rep from * across to last ch-2 sp, sk last ch-2 sp, sc in last sc, change color to wine heather, turn. *(44 [50, 56] sc, 15 [17, 19] ch-2 sps)*

Row 7: Ch 1, sc in first sc, dc in next sk sc 3 rows below, *ch 2, sk next sc, sc in each of next 2 sc, dc in next sk sc 3 rows below, sc in each of next 2 sc, ch 2, sk next sc, dc in next sk sc 3 rows below, rep from * across to last sc, sc in last sc, turn. *(30 [34, 38] sc, 15 [17, 19] dc, 14 [16, 18] ch-2 sps)*

Row 8: Ch 1, sc in each of first 2 sc, *ch 2, sk next ch-2 sp, sc in each of next 5 sts, ch 2, sk next ch-2 sp, sc in next st, rep from * across to last sc, sc in last sc, change color to fog heather, turn. *(45 [51, 57] sc, 14 [16, 18] ch-2 sps)*

Row 9: Ch 1, sc in first sc, *ch 2, sk next sc, dc in next sk sc 3 rows below, sc in each of next 2 sc, ch 2, sk next sc, sc in each of next 2 sc, dc in next sk sc 3 rows below, rep from * across to last 2 sts, ch 2, sk next sc, sc in last sc, turn. *(30 [34, 38] sc, 14 [16, 18] dc, 15 [17, 19] ch-2 sps)*

Row 10: Rep row 6. *(44 [50, 56] sc, 15 [17, 19] ch-2 sps)*

Row 11: Ch 1, sc in first sc, *dc in next sk sc 3 rows below, sc in each of next 2 sc, ch 2, sk next sc, dc in next sk sc 3 rows below, ch 2, sk next sc, sc in each of next 2 sc, rep from * across to last ch-2 sp, dc in next sk sc 3 rows below, sc in last sc, turn. *(30 [34, 38] sc, 15 [17, 19] dc, 14 [16, 18] ch-2 sps)*

Row 12: Rep row 4. *(45 [51, 57] sc, 14 [16, 18] ch-2 sps)*

Row 13: Ch 1, sc in each of first 3 sc, *ch 2, sk next sc, dc in next sk sc 3 rows below, sc in next sc, dc in next sk sc 3 rows below, ch 2, sk next sc, sc in each of next 3 sc, rep from * across, turn. *(31 [35, 39] sc, 14 [16, 18] dc, 14 [16, 18] ch-2 sps)*

Row 14: Rep row 2. *(45 [51, 57] sc, 14 [16, 18] ch-2 sps)*

Row 15: Ch 1, sc in each of first 2 sc, *ch 2, sk next sc, dc in next sk sc 3 rows below, sc in each of next 3 sc, dc in next sk sc 3 rows below, ch 2, sk next sc**, sc in next sc, rep from * across ending last rep at **, sc in each of last 2 sc, turn. *(31 [35, 39] sc, 14 [16, 18] dc, 14 [16, 18] ch-2 sps)*

Row 16: Rep row 8. *(45 [51, 57] sc, 14 [16, 18] ch-2 sps)*

Rows 17–20: Rep rows 9–12. *(45 [51, 57] sc, 14 [16, 18] ch-2 sps at end of row 20)*

Rows 21–24: Rep rows 5–8. *(45 [51, 57] sc, 14 [16, 18] ch-2 sps at end of row 24)*

Row 25: Ch 1, sc in each of first 2 sc, *dc in next sk sc 3 rows below, ch 2, sk next sc, sc in each of next 3 sc, ch 2, sk next sc, dc in next sk sc 3 rows below, sc in next sc, rep from * across to last sc, sc in last sc. turn. *(31 [35, 39] sc, 14 [16, 18] dc, 14 [16, 18] ch-2 sps)*

Row 26: Rep row 2. *(45 [51, 57] sc, 14 [16, 18] ch-2 sps)*

Row 27: Ch 1, sc in each of first 3 sc, *dc in next sk sc 3 rows below, sc in each of next 3 sc, rep from * across, turn. *(45 [51, 57] sc, 14 [16, 18] dc)*

Crown

Size Teen Only
Next row: Ch 1, **sc dec** *(see Stitch Guide)* in first 2 sts, *sc in each of next 18 sts, sc dec in next 2 sts, rep from * once, sc in each rem st, turn. *(56 sc)*

Next row: Ch 1, sc in each sc across, turn.

Rep last row until piece measures approximately 8 inches from bottom edge of Ribbing or 2 inches less than desired height.

Sizes Woman & Man Only
Next row: Ch 1, sc in each sc across, turn. *([67, 75] sc)*

Rep last row until piece measures approximately [9, 9½] inches from bottom edge of Ribbing or 2 inches less than desired height.

Next row: Ch 1, **sc dec** *(see Stitch Guide)* in first 2 sc, *sc in each of next [15, 13] sts, sc dec in next 2 sc, rep from * [2, 3] times, sc in each rem st, turn. *([63, 70] sc)*

All Sizes
Next row (dec): Ch 1, sc dec in first 2 sc, sc in each of next 5 sc, *sc dec in next 2 sc, sc in each of next 5 sc, rep from * across, turn. *(48 [54, 60] sc)*

Next row (dec): Ch 1, sc dec in first 2 sc, sc in each of next 4 sc, *sc dec in next 2 sc, sc in each of next 4 sc, rep from * across, turn. *(40 [45, 50] sc)*

Next row (dec): Ch 1, sc dec in first 2 sc, sc in each of next 3 sc, *sc dec in next 2 sc, sc in each of next 3 sc, rep from * across, turn. *(32 [36, 40] sc)*

Next row (dec): Ch 1, sc dec in first 2 sc, sc in each of next 2 sc, *sc dec in next 2 sc, sc in each of next 2 sc, rep from * across, turn. *(24 [27, 30] sc)*

Next row (dec): Ch 1, sc dec in first 2 sc, sc in next sc, *sc dec in next 2 sc, sc in next sc, rep from * across, turn. *(16 [18, 20] sc)*

Last row (dec): Ch 1, sc dec in first 2 sc, sc in next sc, *sc dec in next 2 sc, sc in next sc, rep from * across, turn. Leaving an 8-inch tail, fasten off. *(8 [9, 10] sc)*

Finishing
Weave tail through last row and pull tightly to secure. Sew back seam. ●

Mosaic Grid Hat

Materials

- Premier Yarns
  Deborah Norville
  Everyday
  Heathers
  medium (worsted) weight
  acrylic yarn (3½ oz/
  180 yds/100g per ball):
  - 1 [1, 2] ball(s) #0007
    cocoa heather
  - 1 ball #0014 terra-
    cotta heather
- Size H/8/5mm crochet
  hook or size needed to
  obtain gauge
- Tapestry needle

Gauge

Ribbing: 4 sc = 1 inch; 13 rows
= 4 inches

Body: 13 sts = 4 inches; 18 rows
= 4 inches

Pattern Notes

Weave in ends as work progresses.

Work all double crochet stitches in
front of chain-2 spaces of previous 2
rows throughout.

Pattern Stitch
Mosaic Grid Pattern

Row 1 (RS): Ch 1, sc in first sc, *ch 2, sk next sc**, sc in
each of next 3 sc, rep from * across, ending last rep at
**, sc in last sc, turn. *(44 [50, 56] sc, 15 [17, 19] ch-2 sps)*

Row 2: Ch 1, sc in first sc, *ch 2, sk next ch-2 sp**, sc in
each of next 3 sts, rep from * across, ending last rep
at **, sc in last sc, change color to cocoa heather, turn.

Row 3: Ch 1, sc in first sc, ***working in front of ch-2
sps of previous 2 rows** *(see Pattern Notes)*, dc in next
sk sc 3 rows below**, ch 2, sk next sc, sc in next sc,
ch 2, sk next sc, rep from * across, ending last rep at

Skill Level

 EASY

Finished Sizes

Instructions given fit teen; changes for woman and
man are in [ ].

Finished Measurements

Circumference: 18 [20½, 23] inches

Length: 10 [11, 11½] inches tall

**, sc in last sc, turn. *(16 [18, 20] sc, 15 [17, 19] dc, 28 [32, 36] ch-2 sps)*

Row 4: Ch 1, sc in each of first 2 sts, *ch 2, sk next ch-2 sp, sc in next st, rep from * across to last sc, sc in last sc, change color to terra-cotta heather, turn. *(31 [35, 39] sc, 28 [32, 36] ch-2 sps)*

Row 5: Ch 1, sc in first sc, *ch 2, sk next sc**, dc in next sk sc 3 rows below, sc in next sc, dc in next sk sc 3 rows below, rep from * across, ending last rep at **, sc in last sc, turn. *(16 [18, 20] sc, 28 [32, 36] dc, 15 [17, 19] ch-2 sps)*

Row 6: Rep row 2.

Row 7: Ch 1, sc in first sc, *dc in next sk sc 3 rows below**, sc in each of next 3 sc, rep from * across, ending last rep at **, sc in last sc, turn. *(44 [50, 56] sc, 15 [17, 19] ch-2 dc)*

Row 8: Ch 1, sc in each st across, change color to terra-cotta heather, turn. *(59 [67, 75] sc)*

Rep rows 1–8 for pattern.

Hat

Ribbing
Row 1 (RS): With cocoa heather, ch 8 [9, 9], sc in 2nd ch from hook and in each ch across, turn. *(7 [8, 8] sc)*

Row 2: Ch 1, sc in **back lp** *(see Stitch Guide)* of each sc across, turn.

Rep row 2 until Ribbing measures 17 [19½, 22] inches, slightly stretched. Do not fasten off.

Body
Foundation row 1 (RS): With RS facing and working in ends of rows, ch 1, work 59 [67, 75] sc evenly sp across, turn. *(59 [67, 75] sc)*

Foundation row 2: Ch 1, sc in each sc across, **change color** *(see Stitch Guide)* in last sc to terra-cotta heather, turn.

Next rows: Work in **Mosaic Grid Pattern** *(see Pattern Stitch)* until piece measures approximately 7 [8, 8] inches from bottom edge of Ribbing, ending at row 8. **Do not change color.**

Crown
Next row: Ch 1, sc in each sc across, turn.

Rep last row until piece measures approximately 8 [9, 9½] inches from bottom edge of Ribbing or 2 inches less than desired height.

Next row: Ch 1, **sc dec** *(see Stitch Guide)* in first 2 sc, *sc in each of next 18 [15, 13] sts, sc dec in next 2 sts, rep from * 1 [2, 3] time(s), sc in each rem st, turn. *(56 [63, 70] sc)*

Next row (dec): Ch 1, sc dec in first 2 sc, sc in each of next 5 sc, *sc dec in next 2 sc, sc in each of next 5 sc, rep from * across, turn. *(48 [54, 60] sc)*

Next row (dec): Ch 1, sc dec in first 2 sc, sc in each of next 4 sc, *sc dec in next 2 sc, sc in each of next 4 sc, rep from * across, turn. *(40 [45, 50] sc)*

Next row (dec): Ch 1, sc dec in first 2 sc, sc in each of next 3 sc, *sc dec in next 2 sc, sc in each of next 3 sc, rep from * across, turn. *(32 [36, 40] sc)*

Next row (dec): Ch 1, sc dec in first 2 sc, sc in each of next 2 sc, *sc dec in next 2 sc, sc in each of next 2 sc, rep from * across, turn. *(24 [27, 30] sc)*

Next row (dec): Ch 1, sc dec in first 2 sc, sc in next sc, *sc dec in next 2 sc, sc in next sc, rep from * across, turn. *(16 [18, 20] sc)*

Last row (dec): Ch 1, sc dec in first 2 sc, sc in next sc, *sc dec in next 2 sc, sc in next sc, rep from * across, turn. Leaving an 8-inch tail, fasten off. *(8 [9, 10] sc)*

Finishing
Weave tail through last row and pull tightly to secure. Sew back seam. ●

Zigzag Hat

Skill Level
 EASY

Finished Sizes
Instructions given fit teen; changes for woman and man are in [ ].

Finished Measurements
Circumference: 18 [20½, 23] inches

Length: 10 [11, 11½ inches tall

Materials
- Premier Yarns Deborah Norville Everyday Soft Worsted medium (worsted) weight acrylic yarn (4 oz/203 yds/113g per ball):
  - 1 [1, 2] ball(s) #1019 navy
  - 1 ball #1022 bittersweet
- Size H/8/5mm crochet hook or size needed to obtain gauge
- Tapestry needle

Gauge
Ribbing: 4 sc = 1 inch; 13 rows = 4 inches

Body: 13 sts = 4 inches; 18 rows = 4 inches

Pattern Notes
Weave in ends as work progresses.

Work all double crochet stitches in front of chain-2 spaces of previous 2 rows throughout.

Pattern Stitches
Zigzag Pattern

Row 1 (RS): Ch 1, sc in first sc, ch 2, sk next sc, sc in next sc, *ch 2, sk next sc, sc in each of next 3 sc, [ch 2, sk next sc, sc in next sc] twice, rep from * across, turn. *(37 [42, 47] sc, 22 [25, 28] ch-2 sps)*

Row 2: Ch 1, sc in first sc, ch 2, sk next ch-2 sp, sc in next sc, *ch 2, sk next ch-2 sp, sc in each of next 3 sc, [ch 2, sk next ch-2 sp, sc in next sc] twice, rep from * across, change color to navy, turn.

Row 3: Ch 1, sc in first sc, ***working in front of ch-2 sps of previous 2 rows** (see Pattern Notes), dc in next sk sc 3 rows below, sc in next sc**, dc in next sk sc 3 rows below, ch 2, sk next sc, sc in next sc, ch 2, sk next sc, dc in next sk sc 3 rows below, sc in next sc, rep from * across, ending last rep at **, turn. *(23 [26, 29] sc, 22 [25, 28] dc, 14 [16, 18] ch-2 sps)*

Row 4: Ch 1, sc in each of first 4 sts, *[ch 2, sk next ch-2 sp, sc in next sc] twice**, sc in each of next 4 sc, rep from * across, ending last rep at **, sc in each of last 3 sc, change color to bittersweet, turn. *(45 [51, 57] sc, 14 [16, 18] ch-2 sps)*

Row 5: Ch 1, sc in first sc, *ch 2, sk next sc**, sc in each of next 2 sc, [dc in next sk sc 3 rows below, sc in next sc] twice, sc in next sc, rep from * across, ending last rep at **, sc in last sc, turn. *(37 [42, 47] sc, 14 [16, 18] dc, 8 [9, 10] ch-2 sps)*

Row 6: Ch 1, sc in first sc, *ch 2, sk next ch-2 sp**, sc in each of next 7 sts, rep from * across, ending last rep at **, sc in last sc, change color to navy, turn. *(51 [58, 65] sc, 8 [9, 10] ch-2 sps)*

Row 7: Ch 1, sc in first sc, *dc in next sk sc 3 rows below**, [ch 2, sk next sc, sc in next sc] 3 times, ch 2, sk next sc, rep from * across, ending last rep at **, sc in last sc, turn. *(23 [26, 29] sc, 8 [9, 10] dc, 28 [32, 36] ch-2 sps)*

Row 8: Ch 1, sc in each of first 2 sts, *ch 2, sk next ch-2 sp, sc in next st, rep from * across to last sc, sc in last sc, change color to bittersweet, turn. *(31 [35, 39] sc, 28 [32, 36] ch-2 sps)*

Row 9: Ch 1, sc in each of first 2 sc, *dc in next sk sc 3 rows below, sc in next sc, rep from * across to last sc, sc in last sc, turn. *(31 [35, 39] sc, 28 [32, 36] dc)*

Row 10: Ch 1, sc in each st across, change color to navy, turn. *(59 [67, 75] sc)*

Hat

Ribbing
Row 1 (RS): With navy, ch 8 [9, 9], sc in 2nd ch from hook and in each ch across, turn. *(7 [8, 8] sc)*

Row 2: Ch 1, sc in **back lp** *(see Stitch Guide)* of each sc across, turn.

Rep row 2 until Ribbing measures 17 [19½, 22] inches, slightly stretched. Do not fasten off.

Body
Foundation row 1 (RS): With RS facing and working in ends of rows, ch 1, work 59 [67, 75] sc evenly sp across, turn. *(59 [67, 75] sc)*

Foundation row 2: Ch 1, sc in each sc across, **change color** *(see Stitch Guide)* in last sc to bittersweet, turn.

Rows 1–10: Work rows 1–10 of **Zigzag Pattern** *(see Pattern Stitches)*.

Rows 11–20: Rep rows 1–10, reversing all color changes. At end of row 20, do not change color.

Crown

Size Teen Only
Next row: Ch 1, **sc dec** *(see Stitch Guide)* in first 2 sts, *sc in each of next 18 sts, sc dec in next 2 sts, rep from * once, sc in each rem st, turn. *(56 sc)*

Next row: Ch 1, sc in each sc across, turn.

Rep last row until piece measures approximately 8 inches from bottom edge of Ribbing or 2 inches less than desired height.

Sizes Woman & Man Only
Next row: Ch 1, sc in each sc across, turn. *([67, 75] sc)*

Rep last row until piece measures approximately [9, 9½] inches from bottom edge of Ribbing or 2 inches less than desired height.

Next row: Ch 1, **sc dec** *(see Stitch Guide)* in first [2, 2] sc, *sc in each of next [15, 13] sts, sc dec in next 2 sc, rep from * [2, 3] times, sc in each rem st, turn. *([63, 70] sc)*

All Sizes
Next row (dec): Ch 1, sc dec in first 2 sc, sc in each of next 5 sc, *sc dec in next 2 sc, sc in each of next 5 sc, rep from * across, turn. *(48 [54, 60] sc)*

Next row (dec): Ch 1, sc dec in first 2 sc, sc in each of next 4 sc, *sc dec in next 2 sc, sc in each of next 4 sc, rep from * across, turn. *(40 [45, 50] sc)*

Next row (dec): Ch 1, sc dec in first 2 sc, sc in each of next 3 sc, *sc dec in next 2 sc, sc in each of next 3 sc, rep from * across, turn. *(32 [36, 40] sc)*

Next row (dec): Ch 1, sc dec in first 2 sc, sc in each of next 2 sc, *sc dec in next 2 sc, sc in each of next 2 sc, rep from * across, turn. *(24 [27, 30] sc)*

Next row (dec): Ch 1, sc dec in first 2 sc, sc in next sc, *sc dec in next 2 sc, sc in next sc, rep from * across, turn. *(16 [18, 20] sc)*

Last row (dec): Ch 1, sc dec in first 2 sc, sc in next sc, *sc dec in next 2 sc, sc in next sc, rep from * across, turn. Leaving an 8-inch tail, fasten off. *(8 [9, 10] sc)*

Finishing

Weave tail through last row and pull tightly to secure. Sew back seam. ●

Annie's®

Learn to Crochet Mosaic Hats is published by Annie's, 306 East Parr Road, Berne, IN 46711. Printed in USA. Copyright © 2016 Annie's. All rights reserved. This publication may not be reproduced in part or in whole without written permission from the publisher.

RETAIL STORES: If you would like to carry this publication or any other Annie's publication, visit AnniesWSL.com.

Every effort has been made to ensure that the instructions in this publication are complete and accurate. We cannot, however, take responsibility for human error, typographical mistakes or variations in individual work. Please visit AnniesCustomerService.com to check for pattern updates.

ISBN: 978-1-59012-647-9

1 2 3 4 5 6 7 8 9

STITCH GUIDE

STITCH ABBREVIATIONS

beg	begin/begins/beginning
bpdc	back post double crochet
bpsc	back post single crochet
bptr	back post treble crochet
CC	contrasting color
ch(s)	chain(s)
ch-	refers to chain or space previously made (i.e., ch-1 space)
ch sp(s)	chain space(s)
cl(s)	cluster(s)
cm	centimeter(s)
dc	double crochet (singular/plural)
dc dec	double crochet 2 or more stitches together, as indicated
dec	decrease/decreases/decreasing
dtr	double treble crochet
ext	extended
fpdc	front post double crochet
fpsc	front post single crochet
fptr	front post treble crochet
g	gram(s)
hdc	half double crochet
hdc dec	half double crochet 2 or more stitches together, as indicated
inc	increase/increases/increasing
lp(s)	loop(s)
MC	main color
mm	millimeter(s)
oz	ounce(s)
pc	popcorn(s)
rem	remain/remains/remaining
rep(s)	repeat(s)
rnd(s)	round(s)
RS	right side
sc	single crochet (singular/plural)
sc dec	single crochet 2 or more stitches together, as indicated
sk	skip/skipped/skipping
sl st(s)	slip stitch(es)
sp(s)	space(s)/spaced
st(s)	stitch(es)
tog	together
tr	treble crochet
trtr	triple treble
WS	wrong side
yd(s)	yard(s)
yo	yarn over

YARN CONVERSION

OUNCES TO GRAMS		GRAMS TO OUNCES	
1	28.4	25	⅞
2	56.7	40	1⅓
3	85.0	50	1¾
4	113.4	100	3½

UNITED STATES		UNITED KINGDOM
sl st (slip stitch)	=	sc (single crochet)
sc (single crochet)	=	dc (double crochet)
hdc (half double crochet)	=	htr (half treble crochet)
dc (double crochet)	=	tr (treble crochet)
tr (treble crochet)	=	dtr (double treble crochet)
dtr (double treble crochet)	=	ttr (triple treble crochet)
skip	=	miss

Reverse single crochet (reverse sc): Ch 1, sk first st, working from left to right, insert hook in next st from front to back, draw up lp on hook, yo and draw through both lps on hook.

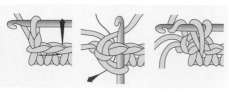

Chain (ch): Yo, pull through lp on hook.

Single crochet (sc): Insert hook in st, yo, pull through st, yo, pull through both lps on hook.

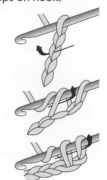

Double crochet (dc): Yo, insert hook in st, yo, pull through st, [yo, pull through 2 lps] twice.

Single crochet decrease (sc dec): (Insert hook, yo, draw lp through) in each of the sts indicated, yo, draw through all lps on hook.

Example of 2-sc dec

Half double crochet decrease (hdc dec): (Yo, insert hook, yo, draw lp through) in each of the sts indicated, yo, draw through all lps on hook.

Example of 2-hdc dec

Front loop (front lp) Back loop (back lp)

Front Loop   Back Loop

Front post stitch (fp): Back post stitch (bp): When working post st, insert hook from right to left around post of st on previous row.

Back   Front

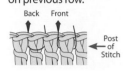

Post of Stitch

Half double crochet (hdc): Yo, insert hook in st, yo, pull through st, yo, pull through all 3 lps on hook.

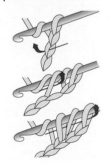

Double treble crochet (dtr): Yo 3 times, insert hook in st, yo, pull through st, [yo, pull through 2 lps] 4 times.

Double crochet decrease (dc dec): (Yo, insert hook, yo, draw lp through, yo, draw through 2 lps on hook) in each of the sts indicated, yo, draw through all lps on hook.

Example of 2-dc dec

Slip stitch (sl st): Insert hook in st, pull through both lps on hook.

Chain color change (ch color change) Yo with new color, draw through last lp on hook.

Double crochet color change (dc color change) Drop first color, yo with new color, draw through last 2 lps of st.

Treble crochet (tr): Yo twice, insert hook in st, yo, pull through st, [yo, pull through 2 lps] 3 times.

Treble crochet decrease (tr dec): Holding back last lp of each st, tr in each of the sts indicated, yo, pull through all lps on hook.

Example of 2-tr dec